P9-DHS-740

for my father

falling asleep

at saint mary's

hospital

Also by Dennis Sampson

The Double Genesis

Forgiveness

Constant Longing

Needlegrass

for my father

falling asleep

at saint mary's

hospital

———————

dennis sampson

MILKWEED EDITIONS

© 2005, Text by Dennis Sampson
All rights reserved. Except for brief quotations in critical articles or reviews,
no part of this book may be reproduced in any manner without prior written
permission from the publisher: Milkweed Editions, 1011 Washington Avenue
South, Suite 300, Minneapolis, Minnesota 55415.
(800) 520-6455 / www.milkweed.org

Published 2005 by Milkweed Editions
Printed in Canada
Cover and interior design by Christian Fünfhausen
The text of this book is set in Filosofia.
05 06 07 08 09   5 4 3 2 1
First Edition

Milkweed Editions, a nonprofit publisher, gratefully acknowledges support
from Emilie and Henry Buchwald; Bush Foundation; Cargill Value Investment;
Timothy and Tara Clark Family Charitable Fund; DeL Corazón Family Fund;
Dougherty Family Foundation; Ecolab Foundation; Joe B. Foster Family
Foundation; General Mills Foundation; Jerome Foundation; Kathleen Jones;
Constance B. Kunin; D. K. Light; Chris and Ann Malecek; McKnight Foundation;
a grant from the Minnesota State Arts Board, through an appropriation by the
Minnesota State Legislature, a grant from the National Endowment for the Arts,
and private funders; Sheila C. Morgan; Laura Jane Musser Fund; an award from
the National Endowment for the Arts, which believes that a great nation deserves
great art; Navarre Corporation; Kate and Stuart Nielsen; Outagamie Charitable
Foundation; Qwest Foundation; Debbie Reynolds; St. Paul Travelers Foundation;
Ellen and Sheldon Sturgis; Surdna Foundation; Target Foundation; Gertrude
Sexton Thompson Charitable Trust (George R.A. Johnson, Trustee); James R.
Thorpe Foundation; Toro Foundation; Weyerhaeuser Family Foundation; and
Xcel Energy Foundation.

Library of Congress Cataloging-in-Publication Data
Sampson, Dennis, 1949–
    For my father falling asleep at Saint Mary's Hospital / Dennis Sampson.—
1st ed.
       p. cm.
    ISBN-13: 978-1-571314-18-5 (pbk. : alk. paper)
    ISBN-10: 1-57131-418-0
    I. Title.
    PS3619.A459F67 2005
    811'.6—dc22

                                                    2004021883

This book is printed on acid-free paper.

NATIONAL ENDOWMENT FOR THE ARTS

MINNESOTA STATE ARTS BOARD

IN MEMORY OF

NORMAN VINCENT SAMPSON,

1913—2001

for my father

falling asleep

at saint mary's

hospital

_____

i n t r o d u c t i o n

IN THE SUMMER OF 2001 MY FATHER BEGAN TO DIE. He had had several sur-
geries, all as a result of prostrate cancer, and had struggled to recover his
health with small success. Now he had taken, as they say, a turn for the
worse. I had just spent several weeks at a writers' colony in Virginia and
had come home on Father's Day to my father getting up and sitting down,
getting up and sitting down at the foot of his bed, trying to master the
simplest of endeavors. My mother sat in the living room, very upset. Who
was this bewildered and tormented man whom she had slept with for over
fifty years and who was behaving so irrationally?

I took him to Saint Mary's Hospital in Pierre, South Dakota, and after
several X-rays the doctor informed both of us that he would have to be
flown immediately to Aberdeen to see a specialist because his cancer had
spread to his spine; if something weren't done soon he could lose his
ability to walk. They flew him in a helicopter—the first trip of that kind
he had ever taken in his life—and I followed behind in his car. I knew his

death was no longer something to be merely imagined. He was scared. And I was scared for him.

The next six months were a journey of extreme importance: he would live, he would die, he would perhaps become a paraplegic. My father returned from surgery hopeful that his life would go on forever. That kind of hope in the dying makes you wonder if you know anything.

I flew back to my house in North Carolina after he had been returned to Saint Mary's Hospital, and thought more ferociously than ever before of what Whitman called "the world's gliding wonders." The particulars of the natural world were never more vivid: a single wren on my windowsill was for me, as that hazelnut was for the medieval English mystic Julian of Norwich, "all that is made." I stared at it with "the eye of my understanding."

In November I flew back up to Minneapolis, after my two dutiful sisters had driven my father and my mother in a huge rented van to a hospital there, where he would live out his final weeks. My mother found assisted-living quarters in an adjoining building. So many hospitals—they all seemed to come together for me in the one identified in the title of this book, located in the prairie town where I was raised.

This is the story of my father's dying and death. It is also the chronicle of my seeing him off in ways I could never have prepared for, and of how a brotherhood was created for me out of what otherwise was simply a concern for the perishable self. It is meant to be read from beginning to end, and with the understanding that not every aspect of the story can be told.

And silent answers crept across the stars.

HART CRANE

for my father

falling asleep

at saint mary's

hospital

I. BEFORE

love of the
ordinary world

(at the Virginia Center for the Creative Arts)

Eyes following Faith up the stairway,

blue wildflowers—"chicory," exclaims Elizabeth when

I ask her—along the path

against a yellow background of tall grass,

Laura Swendinger calling me out into the night

(I left my door wide open)

to see the full moon just above the treeline.

Fireflies. Laura's flute

at morning . . . Father on the phone three days

after his biopsy, too hard of hearing

to comprehend "How are you doing?"

Mother saying: "He's fine,

if I could just get him to use his hearing aid."

Then shadows across the grass

of circling red-tails after the hay's been cut,

tree frogs (two of them)

talking back and forth

in the dusk—first thought to be birds.

♦   ♦   ♦

Can anyone tell me what kind of thistle
this is? No one seems
to know. Faith, on the evening
before she leaves, describes
what it was to be a Buddhist nun,
cobras curled in the lap
of her mentor waking from day-
long meditation. Swendinger's moon ascending.
The shock of my studio when I
turn back to see my desk
illumed in the night. Drizzle.
And that backward glance
by Elissa who does landscape
paintings that look like Fragonard's.

◆   ◆   ◆

In the evenings
I have been reading *Secret Teachings*
in the Art of Japanese Gardens,
gardens with stone lanterns,
pagodas, arched bridges,
at other times nothing but rocks
with names like Hovering Mist,
Cloudlike, Never Aging.
If I were to go to Kyoto and study
with one of the Masters he would no
doubt send me packing,
throwing hands in the air with:
"Go to the pine and don't
come back until you have been
reincarnated at least twice."

So I take my lawn chair
out into the pasture this afternoon
and wait for the sun
to go down—distant mountain,
crows squabbling
as they cross (one in front
drops back and inexplicably trails).
It is sufficient from this chair
when the crow curves up
into the hickory. From here all things
are seen. And what about the life
after life and matters
of like consequence? Tonight's
the solstice, instigating a daydream
in which I remember I always
liked that word, along with "canticle,"
"photosynthesis," "skeleton"—
"brothel," "Telemachus."

◆   ◆   ◆

Before going to bed,
no pleasure looking at photographs anymore
of gardens arranged
with such diligence you could shift
your foot in the sand
and alter them dramatically. My father
far and sick. But I sleep uninterrupted
and wake elated to Laura's flute again.

◆   ◆   ◆

I can't grasp the continuity
of events: where I put
my underpants and who asked who
what "narcosia" meant. The ant
has never ceased investigating
the sweetness my tangerine left
on the table
the morning after Uncle Harlan's
last heart attack. One white miller
among chicory . . .
and I remember a meadow in Alabama
where hundreds of monarchs
shimmered and swayed
to delight my friend and me.
What perfect Japanese garden
could tolerate that? Death less
and less dreadful
the more forgetful I am,
my lying beside Jane in 1997
practicing our dark cantos
with her legs draped over mine,
it just happened didn't it? Ten laps,
backstroke, then Australian crawl,
and I can't catch my breath. Laura
downs her Heineken on the patio,
hoots into the bottle. "That's
the first thing students do
who want to be flutists," she reflects,
then blows again.

♦   ♦   ♦

No stars. But the moon shows through
the overcast around 3 A.M.,
just as I am pissing off the stone steps
of my studio, hiding itself
slyly behind cumulus.
One window in the night
is lit, Sharon Harper
developing her pictures of the planet,
taken from a plane,
which she attaches to her wall
then looks at for the longest time,
critical of their sequence.

                    ◆   ◆   ◆

Even trees like these
need a leader, says the text.
I agree. Maybe it would be
best for one to come forth
gradually—after several seasons.
I misunderstand the meaning
of Boat-Concealing Rocks—
they keep hidden
what's unveiled: boats vanishing
behind isles in "the bay of Akashi."
There are carp to consider,
cyprinid, which tends to be high-
strung, crucian, less temperamental,
the pond dug deeper and with
a floating mat of bamboo
to inspire contentment. In one sketch

a fox is tricked by Frolicking
Birds Rocks that seem to take wing
and a reference to storks
that might alight on eaves is hilarious:
permitted, if there's a pond,
if not (according to Zōen)
"an exorcism must immediately
be performed."

       ✦   ✦   ✦

This evening's slides of Susanne's
paintings in the library cause
all to fall silent: her mother, aunt, others,
molested by the man she calls
"Grandfather," on canvases of vast
width, old photographs
clipped, inserted deep within:
fragile humans. More rain,
then thunder. On page 66
touch is explained
as less important than seeing,
listening relevant to rustling leaves,
falling water, and crickets—taste so low
a priority it's rarely
figured in ("unless, of course,
one actually indulges in a persimmon").
In the shadow of a clipped camellia,
a furtive focal point. It's ridiculous.
In setting out on such an undertaking
two Masters have to be served,

the sensei and, less evident—almost
overlooked—how the garden ultimately
imagines itself, pagoda, no pagoda,
waterfall, wisteria . . .
how appealing a pomegranate
might be. What will become
of me when these "secret teachings"
end and Susanne's *The House*
of Knowledge is taken down,
Sharon's clouds blown away,
tiers of rocks forgotten,
the island overgrown with weeds?
Who will be lead me
now that I am leaving?

◆　　◆　　◆

I wish my father could listen
but he can't, and that's that.
Yet he seems happier than most men
who hear every word that's said,
puttering about his yard in his goofy hat
that keeps the sun from blistering him
with skin cancer he already has.
I have lost the quest. It had
to do with catalogs, didn't it,
bluebird, thistle, hickory,
Gertrud photographing roses
above the railroad trestle in green slacks.
Three pairs of socks are all
I packed, my father and mother

in black and white in this photograph
just after their wedding,
along with Jane at maybe six
on a sofa clasping her hands.
Bach's cello suites. Johnny Cash.
The one candle I have
not lit—my denim quilt. Forget it.
I feel sick. In the end
that we were happy is what matters,
isn't it?—the who what when
of the world forgotten in needlegrass.
At least I remember that.
Would you like to dance?
Come back. Come back.
I have questions I would like to ask
if only you would listen.

going home

Somewhere there is my father. I have to find him.
His name is scrawled in cursive outside the door, above Louie B. Harding,
the name of the man in the last stages
    of Alzheimer's. And when I find him I stop

before that door that is open, for he is asleep, a patch of morphine
affixed just above his shoulder, working. On his side he clutches
his pink blanket, spots of blood
    on the pillow from his raw left ear. His face unshaven, thin.

How frail he is. I could shake him and he would crack.
He summons up for me the sight I had as a child staring down
into a nest high in an ash where fledglings just born
    slept with their fragile eyelids pressed tight. Go in. Touch

his shin. He opens his eyes after a split second and recognizes who I am,
his son—eyes that have traveled so far
to my face. I straighten his pant legs, because he asks
    me to, with a note of exasperation. After he sits up, I give him his glasses.

He has to piss. I hand him the plastic flask after he has slid his sweatpants
to his knees. Watch him urinate without any embarrassment.
Don't take my eyes off his genitals. This could be it. This could be
    what I came to see on the fourth floor of Saint Mary's Hospital

this afternoon in late August. Help him put on the brace, tightening the straps
so when he shifts from the bed to the wheelchair the bones in his lower back
don't disintegrate. Get his filthy white hat. Wheel him
    down the corridor into the elevator after washing his bald head and face

with a warm cloth, out to the car parked before the sign that says PATIENTS ONLY.
My father wants to go home. He wants to sit in his burgundy chair
by the picture window and read
    The Capitol Journal. He wants to carry on that conversation

between husband and wife forever, dialogue of the living woman and man
that speaks of any weather. I have to give in. I have no choice in the matter,
avoiding the pothole in the road that makes him groan,
    the curve taken too sharply, past fields of wild grass on the edge

of town where wind blows across the surface
of the prairie and the sunflowers force their ignorant beauty on us.
Me and my father,
    in silence under the vast sky swept by serried clouds until I come

to the yellow one-story house he has lived in fifty years, sure to back the car into
the driveway so he can make it to the front steps with his walker—
my mother's white blouse flashing
    at the window. Follow him those ten steps, my arms spread. Catch him.

He has lost his balance, panicking in the cramped doorway,
struggling to negotiate around my mother, whom he greets with "Hello, Sweetie."
I have discovered nothing. I have had only intimations . . .
    the fragrance of a woman who leaves a room just as I enter.

Let him sit in his chair. He wants a drink. 7 Up. A little Smirnoff. Two
ice cubes. I get it for him. Turn on the television, the sound low.
And when the talk begins,
        the voice of my mother shouting above the difficulty he has hearing—

the joke she read somewhere, her aside about a neighbor who took two hours
to wash his Buick—I step back. This is the fantastical pantomime of their long
life reenacted. Now he wants to lie down
        in his own small bed. I have been waiting for this, listening. Help him on

with his brace again and follow him in the journey across the carpet to his room.
The brace taken off. Then sleep. My mother has cooked him meat loaf,
scalloped potatoes. Then the voice again. He wants to go
        back to the hospital because he is scared. I hear my mother

say "shit" under her breath and I look over my shoulder to her—this is
her final comment on what death is doing to him. To her. And this
will be repeated
        again and again, smoking one cigarette after the other and never listening

years to come until I am sick of it. To the terrible, the ordinary—
the vicious wind that pouring up from the fields for miles knocks me back.
To death that enters
        with a chisel and hammer and scrapes away unnecessary stone.

On the bed the exquisite sculpted figure glows.

II.   THE CALCULUS OF
      UNEXPLAINABLE
      STRANDS

when i was beginning to
take an interest

in what might come up with something as miraculous as this,
my father bought me a book on spider webs which explains

the calculus of unexplainable strands, arranged
in such a way so that the circle whose center is everywhere

makes perfect sense. Eight-legged dancer, fast on your feet, fooled
at first by grass tossed into your elaborate trap, offended

at being thought an idiot by me,
can you actually travel for miles with the wind?

Great gatherer, what is the reason for your
wanting to position me so correctly?

————

what thoughts of the longing
one calling him

into the listening dark, in the light of the tomb's one door.
What cause stirring his shadow abandoned and broken along the seam
of a wall. What awful process. And why one solid year

screaming behind him like a hawk thrown down from the sky—
his left hand lifted to open the sarcophagus
opening into a country no one wants

for its gleaming teeth, for its unquestionably threadbare art.
What holds us there, closes the inlaid lid, kicks us back out
into the blizzard—is the bird become small. Diminutive flicker

weaving your song, the dead are a river we enter in our sleep
but they are not our dead.
Our dead sit up with us and are a golden impossibility.

———————

give me the turning oak just as the
sun comes through

a clearing in the trees—that monastery, gleaming. I'll take slants
of moonlight too that show a few moths doing what they have to,

that black ant strayed so far it is ascending the blue heaven of my wrist
that I twist up to see. I will not grow sick and tired of wind

in one hickory, not the other, the wren in the middle of her business
that perches for a minute on the sill

and looks at me. Gossamer strung I don't know how from leaf to moving leaf.
Last night the smell of honeysuckle. It was released quickly, and I waited

for what had thrown me back home into the past in Alabama
surrounded by yellow blossoms, my wife slamming the window.

I breathed in their fragrance in narrowing circles—
it haunts the mind. How do you thread, how do you weave?

———————

mother and father in this
photograph look

so young. What a beautiful life she'll have with this man
already bald at thirty. Then here they are, old and sentimental,

ravaged by children and doubt about what to do with a daughter
wanting to borrow money, a restless son who gets drunk

and drives the Pontiac around in the dark. How fragile
they've become after years of being here on this planet,

accepted without questioning—one with a hearing aid, fastidious,
vacuuming and scrubbing, spraying the tabletops with Pledge,

the other refusing to explain about the knee that makes her wince
when she's just sitting. Their lives are so intertwined

separation through death would be a crime. And yet one must go—
the other struggle briefly to survive.

———————

when the crows start up with me
this morning

I scrape back my chair, run out onto the patio
with something to cast up into the branches:

my can of beets, my coffee cup, my dull Bible.
I plunge my face into my pillows.

I beseech the gods for a little peace.
I curse their cajoling, their infinite screams,

let myself be provoked by the politician of the mulberry—
tormented by the critic of small pleas. I exclaim,

Let me sleep Let me sleep And that crow
answers back: *You will, and for longer than you think.*

———

i will die alone in my house

and they'll cart my body off
to the morgue at Vogler's Funeral Home
to stiffen between the stenographer withered to a stick

and the bricklayer with one blind eye. The autopsy report
will show that I smoked and drank to excess.
Pork hardened the arteries.

But nothing will be said of the eviscerating dream
of being chased by a gorilla through the Lutheran church,
my hours of failure in marriage. My fear of heights.

Out to the hearse the story I never wrote
will go with me into the ceremony arranged to explain it all,
with the salt wash of the sea and gulls borne upward

through the sky on unmoving wings.

———

morning crow, demanding so much
of the world again,

your loud pronouncements along the illuminated upper reaches
of that withered sycamore across the street, darkened by last night's drizzle,
are not needed. Nothing to be gained sounding your black caw,

as you do as if trying to convert me before slanting off to join
those other barbarians, your brothers,
who have made life miserable for the bobolink. In you is the reconciliation

I seek with the ballet of the cardinals, paired for life in their bewildering fidelity,
accumulating above the funeral procession approaching the mausoleum
as if curious, belligerent—always in the chase. A pact with you. Go on being

who you are and leave me to sit and think. We have quarreled enough.
Surely you can see what you want is yours for the taking.

———

this evening a candle

bought from Sears, lit with difficulty, and it's Alighieri. See
how he fears his fall from grace to the acknowledgment everything

he thought remarkable about the universe has its flip side? Blue within
light-blue shimmering the silhouette of its iridescence, this candle seems to ask,

"Should I purge myself of everything that permitted me to live at a distance?"
Nel mezzo del camin di nostra vita . . . when I get up to get another Bud Lite.

Bowing as if in deference to my departure from the path of truth,
it averts its stare—midway in the journey of my life—

straightens, trembles again, is still,
the slightest chill blown down from the heavens.

———————

the night the comet finally slipped into view

over the plains,
incomprehensible time

leading up to this long performance across the sky,
it flashed through the cosmos.

What needed to be uttered
was too far back to be summoned all this distance to the tongue.

"God," said my father.
"Good Lord," said my mother against the cold.

And I turned over in my mind a wild idea, beyond what sanctified this night,
the comet steering inward along the heart then veering off—

having come so far so slowly for so long.
I reveled in the emptiness left behind.

—————

i w o n d e r w h a t i t t a k e s

to determine what the sun is doing in a field of golden wheat,
why night hands itself off to dawn repeatedly, and all the mockingbirds
teasing the world seem always the first. It is not betrayal of love that changes

from day to day like autumn on a stream, that slow cloud-drift over Eagle Butte
along the magnificent honesty of evening
as much mine as that lark uncontrollably singing. Be nothing.

Know nothing. Empty of every feeling.
Stare down at the shadow at your feet. You can't take it with you
any more than you can wish it away.

—————

i s e e n o w, b u t i c a n ' t r e a l l y s a y

what lies at the center of what I celebrate, first frost on the lawn,
and the sudden appearance of a beagle belonging to the retired bricklayer

clearing branches from his gutter up the street, a wanderer through
my living room, Diogenes incognito, as if this were the only way to behave

and be happy. I am honored and amazed
this day in late October is given effortlessly and allowed a little breeze,

a reprieve that darkens, each tree needful, considering what this means,
then regains its gleam and shames the cynic in me with,

O purity of all earth, how could it be any other way? I cannot speak of the origin
of all creation, of what, if anything, claims the iridescence of a mud-dauber,

perplexed by my windowpane, that I trap inside a glass and set free.
What does not want to be known cannot be named.

———————

death, that old complaint,

so misunderstood, carrying his inevitable coffin,
might fall silent in the wake of such a simple expression—a sentence

that needs no embellishment—because he too is loved beyond his fame,
because the half-moon shines on the wave, because the song of sorrow

got it wrong, because you had the decency to include him—one sentence
said directly whose syntax approximates that lacework of black branches

against a sky at twilight quickly diminishing. Let it be curves
of silvering needlegrass on a hillside in South Dakota driven by the breeze,

where the evanescent shadow of a sole cloud stays. And geldings graze
next to a barn outside Woonsocket abandoned to wind and rain and
    mysterious sleet.

———————

i will not creep with the recently deceased

or crawl into my grave with my litanies and proclaim. The mockingbird
has come down from its high place in the Japanese maple to strut

among its brethren, flashing that long white tail that betrays its impatience,
senator of the platitudinous utterance, a fake that in finally finding

just the right note deceives the world and still seems certain
of who it isn't. I like the identifiable song,

that of the chickadee, the devilish mockingbird's pleasure. I will not draw
the parentheses of every day around me and anticipate the eulogy

of the whippoorwill which, when it chooses to,
simply gives up on us, apologetically—and moves through the poplars.

----

black widow, in the predawn

streaked with an arabesque of paint, hole in winter into which I gaze,
in your negligee of cobwebs abandoned long ago by the industrious little

money-lenders that spin in another place. Abyss of the open mouth
in sleep. Monotonous night. And this inquisitive lifting of a veil

light as ether to affirm the culmination of a face we thought we knew,
unknown. Where did it flee? And where will we look for it from here on in?

----

a cricket kept me up all night

confined to a crevice in the fireplace—disgruntled desert father
that has figured out at least he can sing, if not eat, consoling himself
with the sound of his own making. It continues its sweet supplication

as I run my hands under the tap after breakfast, splash my face.
In a house on the plains
my mother feels this sunlight on her face waking to the radio

and my father too, folded in sleep. What shame is there in imagining
the canticle of a cricket in a fireplace
that does not know any better, working to change what we need?

Something about the dawn. That's what I wanted.
Something that tips the scales for us—that balances the disgust.

———————

shadows in forsyth cemetery
i pass this morning

to the tune of *Bobby McGee*, belted out by Janis in '68.
Long unwavering darknessess on Halloween. October cast across the ponds.

Those bold headstones, mottled by sunlight.
As well as that gravedigger waist-high in a new one by the highway

laboring with a shovel, flinging the dirt.
And I'm reminded of this in my office when I turn

from a freshman essay on Emily Dickinson's dread of the inevitable—
and *cannot see to see.* For just one moment I do not think about the pain,

my father taking his medication, getting into bed with help from an aide.
Shadows. And at the stern of that great freighter rocking the dead to sleep,

creaking, under inexplicable orders to stay where it is,
this image of gravel being hurled as if by no one, golden, circumscribing the sky.

Turn out the light. Go to Coltrane
as if he were epithalamium—as if he were elegy.

———————

out of nowhere, the orb-weaver descends,

released after thorough questioning, drags its thread with spinnerets
spooling it out, reaches another tree. Deftly ascends. The gossamer

you see when the light of the sun strikes it
is all the explanation you will ever need. And the Cynthia moth

quivers in my palm. And the house sparrow that found the slightest
opening in my window flings

through the room, a seraph that mistakenly veered left, looked around,
surmised immediately: *Why this is hell, nor am I out of it.*

I'd like to know what accounts for the live oak I love above all others
that has lost its leaves, those blue unnamed wildflowers

I diligently inspected on my knees before my reading last February.
You can have the apocalypse, the politician

who steps up to the podium to expostulate. Far away my father,
closer my mother. This is the way it is for me.

———————

across the screen, blind, in
monday's last light

a caterpillar crawls, in no hurry, just above my eye. It is an exploration
in good faith which fascinates, and I note in this journal

given to me by my sister its obliviousness to my father
rolled over on his side who has to have his diaper changed

in a hospital in Aberdeen; to the newlywed slugged by her husband,
to starlight over the Aegean, to the North Sea, to the blue eyes of a child

opening on a scrawl of starlings on the lawn: obliviousness to everything.
Have I made too much of the trouble that besets a father and son

in this life we live, writing down the spectacle of a caterpillar,
drawing analogies? In complete dark I see its silhouette, the lifting of its head.

Sympathy lies at the heart of meaningless struggle.

———————

in the dark, always my desire

always my dream of a finger along the inner thigh and the human scent.
What loves me is loved. And this is as it should be:
sharp peak of the collar bone and the sundering I idealize

on a Tuesday night when thunder turns northeast over Winston-Salem
and a siren from far away screams the story of grief, of the end of a life
among so many—old metal-worker slumped over in his recliner.

You have to figure the rest out in your dream within this sleep,
within this coupling. Touch not mine. Tenderness someone else's. Kiss.
Sacred the look into another's eyes at night.

Sacred the shuddering evening. This sleep that is mine,
that is granted—and gratefully received.

———

when summer returns for a
day this november

to see how dark it is in the yards, I discover
the several spider webs all woven after midnight
around the old and able evergreens lining the final length of road

on Lake Forest Drive. Too numerous to count, no wider than my palm,
they twist bewilderingly inward
gown after gown. They are still wet with dew at seven o'clock.

It is the sheer quantity that gives me pause. Might there not be
for all these unseen architects enough of lacewing, moth, to go around?—
and then I wonder what is going on, my eye bent upon the privacy of one,

within this mind that's organized along with so many others this spectacular
wedding gown in the sun. What abides together
abides apart. I get lost, am turned around. Have I not found

the ephemeral spider web in the dawn
and written down in longhand symbol, sign? Something for everyone?

———————

the apple tree in november twilight
can sleep now

her journey over for a season
(she did not seem to be moving, but she was).

With her humming with bees I followed her all the way.
First the girl averting her gaze, ashamed,

then her infatuation in April and the shawl of blossoms,
ceremony of her long silence after three days of rain.

I remember the dignity of her deliberations,
how she shook day after day when the downpour

insinuated perfect beauty was a waste.
How she appeared in profile, transfiguring light and shade.

Then the sudden coming together under cover of night,
which I missed (yet imagine against her wishes),

withdrawal into contemplation, a windless shape—blameless.
The worry. And her giving birth.

And the pride she surely took in holding on—
whisperings untranslatable to the visitor in his leather jacket

who stared up at her. Where have you loved?
What are the words for what you have done so skillfully?

I have learned purpose and endured.

————

when i lifted my father out of
his hospital bed

and arranged him in his wheelchair
wind sang in the green field, caressing a piece of cellophane entangled
in a fence line above the Missouri River. The uncomprehending sky

had nothing else to witness when I carried him
so he could sit awhile in his burgundy chair
overlooking Robinson Street, small, bewildered. A father

in your arms is a promise kept: valediction of sage, rage of sunflower,
needlegrass and blizzard—
the oncologist who looks you frighteningly straight in the face.

Hawks circling so high you think you yourself are drifting.
I will go to the river in the night and wait for the dawn that appeared
beneath a door when I was seven.

I will refuse to move until that light is given.

III.   TO ENTER THE
MIND OF ONE
YOU LOVE

a doe draws slowly out
with its head up

then browses clover along a stream
until the hunter and the hunted stand
face to face—you know the rest
of the story: the bolt out of dappled sunlight,
the *crack*, a trail of blood zigzagging
for half a mile, then the pursuit through
thick undergrowth and the question:
How in the world did this come to pass?

This doesn't count
for much in the mind's fantastic
pantomime of paired images bent to their meal
at a long table, the nightshirt lifted
over the head—the heart in hiding. Here.
You can have the story of Abraham
which has nothing to do with love, the glittering
blade slitting open the throat for a voice.
Grip the handle. Pull.
It is the law. A ruthless god exists.

I drove all summer through prairie grass
watching the endless rise and fall
of blackbirds above the corn, certain the origin of

and simple answer to my longing lay
like a triangle of sunlight on far stilled water.
Past farmhouses, shelterbelts, bluffs,
I leaned into the wheel and encouraged
the little surgeon of a single thought
to do its work, cutting and stitching.
Then the startled exclamation. Then the metaphor

frayed, knitted together again,
the raveled skein spread on a tablecloth
in absolute blackness, with the only light to see by
a light that issued from the mind's
amusement at how everything was the same,
a sweep of cottonwoods
beside a creek bed north of Hayes,
the dragon no different than a wildflower.
The face a map, fingers a catacomb of scars.

IV. THE INITIATION OF ANOTHER DAY

———

"Mercy" said Lean. And then he was moved by some violence of feeling, for he turned suddenly upon his two men and tigerishly said, "Throw the dirt in."

— STEPHEN CRANE, *"The Upturned Face"*

what do you write about?

she asked. Did she mean Uncle Bob going out for the pass
one afternoon after he had drunk gin and tonics for an hour in the sun,
his white legs flashing, his face so fierce you'd think his life depended
on the ball that flew through his hands?

Or did she mean that sickle moon of a scar above the eyebrow
where my nine-iron caught my father on my back swing
when he was trying to teach me how to chip by keeping my elbows in?

"What do you write about?" she asked, spiders, flowers, caskets.
The pleasure that comes from contemplating death, I almost said.
And out of desperation I remembered the sea, working out its pathological

longings. And sought what was left of a rainbow reaching erotically
across the water. In the silence,
I answered: "Children love to be chased by someone they trust."

                                    ✦   ✦   ✦

Snow fell at twilight, gently, just enough to cover the shrubs
and lawns. I'd come home right after class to walk the dog and found
myself humming in the car. I must have been happy.

In the mailbox no letter but a message on the answering machine
kept me wondering all the way down Lake Forest Drive to the pond:
Someone who loved me wanted to know if I was doing alright.

Snow ceased, wind stilled—the streetlights stuttered on.
Was I happy? I hadn't thought about it until I caught myself humming
and didn't care one way or another if there was a letter.

———————

i did not capture the hurrying nurse,
the neurologist

who crawled up into the bed
to wrench the exhausted self back into the chest.
I did not capture the wringing hands. That whimper.
So in lieu of this I snapped photographs
of my father facing away from the drapery
holding open his eighty-eight-year-old mouth
to take in the gruel I spooned. I even knelt once

to memorialize his dour countenance on the pillow
in silhouette—light from the east window.
I did not get transcendence
and concealed my camera cupping it
when Sister Madeline in street clothes touched my father long
on the forehead, saying a blessing.
And my father shut his eyes and moved his lips
as she tapped him, twice,
with her pen on his temple when she was finished.

I did not get the soliloquy, the blurted confession,
the cry for water at the last minute.
Instead I got the mountain range of bones
in the deserted landscape of his hand

at the foot of which a Bedouin in black,
half asleep, rocked in a rhythm that possessed him.

I caught the seam where the eyelids came together,
indecipherable whisperings, words spoken to the night,
liver spots on the head, blemishes,
spittle spreading like cobwebs between his lips
when he spoke of the drunken clarinetist from Chamberlain
in a dance band in '46. I got the tongue
of rich remembrance, the stiffening fist.

I did not capture the letting go—
that imperceptible surrender. If I had
I would have seen a graveyard glittering like
rotten teeth in the mist, mausoleum in late winter,
angle of sunlight on snowdrifts,
perspective of bluffs ethereal in the distance.

And nothing prepared me for those
eyes that broke me in half—
that's what I got—opening inwardly.
They looked at me from across the room.
Hold that pose. Don't flinch. I got that.
Slack flesh. Purple veins of the calf.
What I got I gave back.

———

look, i don't say to my father,

there are the stars in a cloudless sky, the moon
at its crescent; there is the drifting night itself,

and the yellow crocuses
under the sycamore in beginning spring.

Look, I don't say, pointing at the dawn
driven by the sun that's yet

to crest the trees, there
is the initiation of another day,

the star of Lucifer, the fading moon,
streaks that waken the wren.

See, taking his hand,
these are the astonishingly long fingers

that danced on the keys
of the saxophone and made it sing,

the bones and ligaments
that strained, the heart that took it all in.

And this my love for you coming out like wind
into the clearing, that cannot help me, rippling the long grass

at twilight where for the first time we observe
the world together without fear.

---

come said the night, and i will
fold my wings around you,

come of the darkness and listen to my song.
Away from the river that flows nowhere.
Away from the darkness with me now.

Come said the silence, I will shelter you,
out of your sanctuary of blue and yellow flowers.
Come of the wind and rain and sleet.
Touch this hand outstretched to you now.

Come of the clearness. Understand my sorrow.
Come of the mystery and welcome me in the dawn.
Come of the world. I will be yours
along with that sun, with that moon—and those many stars.

———————

the radiologist sticking up bone scans
on the screen, floating clouds

of dust—Serpens Nebula with its rearing head, Ursa Major,
a universe flecked with pinpricks, anthropological interpretations,
pathetic fallacies . . . yes.

This one looks exactly like Benito Mussolini just before he was
hung up by his heels
in the Piazzale Loreto, mistress clinging to his sleeve, arms crossed,
chin up. Death walks this splendid plaza with something on his conscience.

Death with his big ideas. His busywork and his pins.

———————

i like the eloquence of the dead

what the prairie keeps expressing to the desert. Desperate virgin
and stupid thief, in the end what goes on living in the song of sorrow
isn't the body, for God's sake. Surely you can see that's so much bullshit.

It's the banter, eternal monologue of the aficionado
standing with his pants down and his middle finger fiddling
up around inside his rectum for the ultimate answer.

That has to be comprehended for the deepest reason, forgotten
in an instant, in unlistening stillness beside the kidney. Who
put it there. And why, where it is so hard to extract?

————

come back

says the odor of a single rose. It trembles like a touched piano
in the dusk. Hocus-pocus. Rises toward you in a gust. And no it does

not obliterate. It constructs. This is the generosity of the end of life.
Red-winged blackbird on a fence post. Stay with the scent of brome.

Fragrance of black grief. Come back to death, which cannot tell the two
of you apart. The mind is an unnecessary sentinel. I say this now,

as if I lived, as if I knew the truth and lived, the truth of bindweed,
the landscape of the prairie. Come back, slick, supercilious—just like the cat.

————

the night the phone rang in my
room at the ramada

I knew it was you. Out of what disastrous darkness of beating wings
did I reach and from where was I fleeing when I heard
the amiable nurse state simply, "Your father wants to see you"?

I think it was the kingdom of the unredeemed, the loathing
of the dark and void—souls wild-eyed,
propelled by a gale they themselves had created. I think it was just sleep.

And I slowed my car at the hospital, staring up wonderingly
at your window. Fourth floor. Second from the left.
Light off. In the dark on your side you lay there waiting, waiting.

———

according to our dead

relentless in their concrete crypts and a little embarrassed
at how they are portrayed, with long white manes and long fingernails
and a grin that scares the bejesus out of even the fiercest believer,

there is this ladder in the afterlife up which one climbs eternally.
You can smell talcum mixed with analgesic on the blunderer
in front and hear the heavy breathing of the blunderer stumbling behind,

while a chorus, unseen, sings so screechingly you can't hear
yourself think. This is their testimony, definitely,

written in the *Book of Wisdom.* With invisible ink. Which I
have figured out. I the phantom
of the nightly drink—the true ghoul. No use to talk to me.

———————

pre-op, snow falling, nighttime,
and my father whispers

from his pillow, "I'm concerned."

"I know," I say.

"Do you think I should go through with this?"

"You have to."

"It's just that I'm concerned."

"You'll be okay."

"You think so? You'll be there?"

"I'll be there."

"As long as you're going to be there."

———————

impresario of the old unknown

crucifixion of widow, black root,
marl and muck, insidious pit

of millipede, slug, and beetle.
Waste and welter. Hissing hair.
Pandemonium of kettledrum, cymbal.

By way of the ditch, by way of the culvert,
go, by way of the grave
keeping its secrets, those clean bones,
skull, clavicle, vertebrae, and teeth,
by way of the worm,
agitation of bats blowing past.
By way of the howl, the shriek.

---

the only thing worth worrying about

is the deceased, who neither care nor reject
our blessings, fed up with constantly setting the record straight.
They are borne stolidly through the black sky this night

above the grain elevator in Aberdeen. If only I had known this.
And I should have listened to the sinister voice that spoke of the everlasting
on my radio in the basement in 1963, my eyes wide to the ceiling. It comes

to me again, murmuring into my ear like a loving conspirator.
I listen like a spy who raises a finger to his lips and looks around. Moon
over Birmingham, moon over Rapid City—moon over Aberdeen,

shedding perfection on the water meadow with wind
across blue reeds. Moon over Mecca, Jerusalem, Kansas City,
lift up. Let me see your fist. Something unendurable is coming.

---

and yet on this morning i find you

on the edge of your bed, in your plaid slacks, laughing,
shaken loose from that unassailable eternity always at a loss for words

that has hurled you back, clear-minded as the November sunlight
blooming in your window. I wheel you down for breakfast. You recognize

everyone, lifting your green felt slippers just above the linoleum
demanding "Go faster," then sit at a long table with unsmiling others,

regal even as you gulp your coffee, devour your grits.
Old prophet grimacing, turning your ear so you can listen,

where have you been? How have you come to be like this
before death, ravenous—as if there were never enough—

running your forefinger over the plate you then kiss with your lips?

———————

night pulls down its shimmering
anklebone of a moon

across the hospital above the veterans' cemetery. The woman
in her wheelchair under the awning shouts out, "I don't believe that
anymore. It's ashes to ashes. Dust to dust." She knows,

a crone among other fugitives circling to smoke and converse
above the roar of the city bus grinding up Bryant Drive.
Orderlies and nurses, their shifts finished, bend against the chill.

Shouldn't it be blizzarding? A sky so clear
I see the windows of a 737 up there on its final approach sliding down,
letting the dead know the living are just as pitiless as ever.

Appreciate, in your vigil, the overhead light left on to read
the final paragraph about who cheated on whom—
how to make a salad out of tulips—strategies to overcome claustrophobia.

Enter the revolving door, glance sideways at that savage crone
flicking ashes, still hollering above the abyss
that follows you up the elevator to the fourth floor

where your father lives. Mouth hung open, he strains to say the unsayable.

———————

what i know of the one truth can be found
in a rose, the american beauty

wordless outside my father's house—a gift for the new millennium.
Blight wore it down—a soul suffering alone. And water brought it back
to the care of a hand. He bore witness to the resurrection
getting up out of his chair and just staring down. What I know

rises, levels out like wood smoke, a smear of frost on a windowpane
guided by the fingertip of a child. Disappears. Or takes its bright orange ball
and walks off sobbing into the twilight, vindictive,
throwing itself into the arms of a mother in her open bathrobe.

What I know, in sunlight over a house in South Dakota, at the beginning
of winter, slams shut. Accepts the cold. Says *No further scrutiny*. Digs in,

glistening with dew. And laughs uproariously at the one lie.
What I know fits neatly on the head of a pin.

———————

in a room that is no longer a room

where there is no light to see by, no light to touch,
in the opening hand a silence lurks, to which a shadow shaped

like a shriven bird fastens itself. And will not let me rest. Your eyes,
if they held water, would not spill. Your mouth, if it were parted,

could not speak. A ruin of threaded straw has grown up around this shadow
that stands between the mystery beginning and the mystery finished. There,

in fiery darkness, leaves are spiraling into the silence of *otherwise*
and *there*. A cricket sings the only prayer.

And the one clear truth takes possession of both of us.

———————

one step, then another, i don't look up

until, loose in the tent, a sparrow wheeling around
my head finds daylight and I almost slip
gripping the pole that wobbles and bends.

I am perfection in the end
walking out across this vast arena,
caught in the spotlight's glare. And all

the faces gazing up are lost in the intensity of this event,
projecting my arrogant leg like a cat's, then lying back
on this high-wire tightened to accept

the weight of a man. I am exhausted from going as slow
as I can, the clowns rushing out when I am done,
doing somersaults, pirouettes.

Then I remember my hesitation, stock-still, leg lifted,
when the sparrow flashed
between my beginning and my end
and I held my breath. And was myself again.

---

in the silence the young indian
orderly danaught

shaves you, changes your blood-stained sheets. A blonde towel
is tucked up under your chin to support your jaw. This is for your wife
who will sit with you by the crimson lampshade—one hand over the other.
In her frayed cardigan sweater, in her gray corduroy pants, she kisses

you on the brow when she comes in, then stands awhile
over your bedrail looking into your far eyes that no longer recognize,
no longer want anything to do with this brown world.
Death takes our breath away; endless. Without cause.

Incredible the way the dead demonstrate how powerful they are,
their future contained within an expressionless brow,
superior even to the wildest sorrow. To laying on of hands, to libations.
Forget them. Forget this moment in desperate November, one person

speaking to another. What brought the two of you to this moment
is what counts. Carry a candle to the cold balcony and watch the sputtering
flame go out, into this windlessness that includes the evening star.

———————

there is a cold god

who longs for deserts too and turns away from no one,
where the soul, no longer certain of anything,
simply listens to the emptiness of wind and sand—
where the sky at night
never loses its blue and the breath of night-blooming cactus

perfumes the air. I would like to go there with faith in myself,
reading under the leaves of palms occupied by cockatoos,
a place where no one dares intrude
even when I dream of other humans.
Who knows what truth might ruin me as I kneel at still pools

lifting my eyes to every evening sky? At night, when I am frightened
and feel the need for further reassurance,
I would listen to wind unimpeded by anything resembling trees
or dwellings: a howl hurdling over the dunes, a hush—
a heaven of constellations.
How beautiful this search for sanctity now seems to me.

St. Jerome in penitence tells the story
at the mouth of a cave when he looks up and away and is purified
by what is lovely. Where is the source of his forgiving grace?

Andromeda right above my head tonight, the Seven Sisters,
I remember again that frantic hour at the hospital in Aberdeen
that has no bearing on what is,
what was. On what is sure to come. My blessing was the touch.
Small wonder it took me a lifetime to figure that one out.

———————

i have always wanted to begin

with giving the river the first and last word, lay down the law,
walk out of my body, the wind, meticulous, searching the vermillion

of a far meadow north of Mobridge for something hidden. To give up
this goddamn shadow that answers to no one, find my father beyond

his trying, wind whipping his hat off as he pisses into a ditch.
I would lift his bare foot again with both hands, remember how little he cared

for the elegance of a western sky wreathing yellow into red
(it could break the heart of a horse)—and cup his ankle. But the ordinary

eyes of the returning close. The dead, dirt poor, just stop receiving.
During the apocalypse the river continues carrying its driftwood to the sea.

———————

have i made you live

in the longing of these words? I tell myself you are somewhere else.
Turn. You are here in your orange Bermuda shorts, drifting into the living room

from clipping the hedge, sweating, saying to your beloved
in her blue armchair, "These bugs aren't biting
like they're supposed to"—or pacing the floor opening forbidden drawers

just after your brother's coronary. In following after knowledge—
such as it was—I heard the aria in the field, the hoot of two barred owls
who knew where I was in the dark
and liked that darkness, that distance—that wide disguise.

I want the solo you mastered on your clarinet, *Harlem Nocturne*,
to be remembered this night of nurses furtive in the hall, solicitous—ethereal.
Artie Shaw, Pete Fountain . . . a lullaby that lets you go with grace.

This will not be given. Not even to me.

———————

hardly a moment passes. then poof

floating daylilies in the yard. And that mathematical whiz
of a garden spider corrects its web, frayed overnight, working furiously
before retiring to speculate and connive.
Addicted to touch it loves the fluttering miller.

In memory I find you again, childlike, tearing yourself away, saying,
after surgery, "Admit it. I look like shit."—from this presentation
of another season, listening to the 23rd psalm
spoken awkwardly by your daughter in the night-light of your bedroom.

Inconsolable, I say what the river says. In which all verities exist. I persuade
with the tabernacle of a daylily darkened by shade, that golden bee.

What remains remains. And is unchangeable.
Just ask that spider over there. That miller.

———————

somewhere out there, tapping,
deep in the trees

before passing on what is certainly its love of the literal,
the woodpecker communicates with me, leaning out my window.
What are you insisting? Suddenly nearer, turning its gaze on grass that fades,

biblical wildflowers that wither (*Ecclesiastes* strides again through weeds
and fallen leaves), tapping, tapping—just above my upturned face
twisting to locate it in the hickory, now upside down, now sideways, in the ash,

in the apple . . . Shameless messenger you are pleading your case,
saying, in so many words: bereft in the temple, in the ditch, in the difficult city,
everything is not horror, but joy.

———————

in fall i hear the cry

from the stadium surrounded by an aura of blue light
just as the boy breaks free of the final tackler
and the man who is his father rises,
quieter than everyone else, in his green windbreaker,
his rolled-up program raised to shield his eyes.

In fall the turned-over field yields to the bark
of a golden retriever, on his haunches

at that threshold that stops with the dark.
He wants to be called, swept into the kitchen,
told to go lie down. He looks over his shoulder.
Goes on barking half-heartedly when no one responds.

Then it is November. The retiree three houses down
rakes leaves toward his bonfire in the dark of Monday night,
at times, when he nears the blaze, a specter—
laboring with something he cannot do without.
In winter my mother spins around
in her threadbare chair and watches a commercial airliner

drift through the clouds. The sorrow she thought she had
figured out gives in to the sorrow that lifts,
in an updraft, the oldest tree in the yard.
In winter the transience of life—
the letting go of all that loved what it was.
What happened to that serious pact with summer

to love the world no matter what the price,
love the questions, touch and be touched—
to the nightly prayer for the voice that is like no other?
What happened to the vow not to drink alone,
and what was going through your mind
when you coaxed a white moth up into a paper cup

one night when you were drunk? To let things flow by,
forget death, focus on fellowship and suppress

your hatred of the cat next door that stalked
and crouched, stalked and crouched,
hunting the cardinal an hour before dusk
before withdrawing to contemplate its loss?

Now wind. Now rain. Now sleet in the Japanese maple
thrashing about. And you with your new resolve
to get up, change what you've become, swallow your pride.
Impossible. Let it be said you had pity on a moth
who bore no other gift to give
to the thoughtless creature of a summer night.

for the coming of winter
under the hunter

"What are you doing down there?"
    my mother asked, and from the depths
        of the basement my father answered, "Working!"
            And while she never seemed quite satisfied
        with this, she'd go about her business
            clearing the table of its wreckage,
plates and silverware, while we watched *Rawhide.*

    Drifting to sleep, my mother gone to bed,
        I'd listen to him climb the stairs,
            to the click of one light after the other
                and the clatter of coins on his dresser. "What
            were you doing down there?" my mother asked,
                gently now, and he said "Working"
in a voice so melancholy it filled me with fear.

    Many Christmases have vanished
        without any revelation of my father's intent
            as he bent to whatever was at hand,
                no extraordinary machine of ropes and pulleys
            grotesque on the dining-room floor. Tonight
                I remember my ex-wife
above the chorus of children's screams in 1989,

"What are you doing down there?"
and look up suddenly
   from my sanctuary of a story
      my father would have had trouble understanding,
   waiting for him to say
      after a pause timed perfectly, "Working" —
working on a past I only imagined might be redeemed.

V.   EPILOGUE

sing to me. i don't have the strength

to do anything but sit here and listen. Lay your bald head on my lap
if you wish. This is your death and I don't want to insist
if you can't handle this. Nevertheless a little jingle
would be pleasing: mumbled, hummed, a note or two or three.

When you are finished and the sleep we need (flickering with lightning perhaps)
slides like a girl on ice up to the steps of the little red schoolhouse outside
   Woonsocket,
what you hummed and what I thought you hummed will come together.

Nothing prepared me for you.

a c k n o w l e d g m e n t s

Some of the poems in this volume first appeared—at times in different versions—
in the *American Scholar*, the *American Voice*, the *Hudson Review*, and on the Poet of
the Month Web site (http://members.aol.com/poetrynet/month/).

DENNIS SAMPSON was born and raised in South Dakota. He is the author of four books of poetry, the most recent being *Needlegrass* (Carnegie-Mellon University Press), and he has published individual poems in such places as *Poetry Northwest*, *Ploughshares*, the *Hudson Review*, *Ohio Review*, *Third Coast*, and the *American Scholar*. From 1996 to 1998 he was Writer-in-Residence at Sweet Briar College in Virginia and later in the MFA program at the University of North Carolina, Wilmington. Since 2000 he has lived in Winston-Salem, where he teaches at Wake Forest University.

MORE POETRY FROM

MILKWEED EDITIONS

To order books or for more information, contact
Milkweed at (800) 520-6455 or visit our Web
site (www.milkweed.org).

Turning Over the Earth
Ralph Black

Morning Earth:
Field Notes in Poetry
John Caddy

The Phoenix Gone, The Terrace Empty
Marilyn Chin

Twin Sons of Different Mirrors
Jack Driscoll and Bill Meissner

Invisible Horses
Patricia Goedicke

The Art of Writing:
Lu Chi's Wen Fu
Translated from the Chinese
by Sam Hamill

Playing the Black Piano
Bill Holm

Butterfly Effect
Harry Humes

Good Heart
Deborah Keenan

The Long Experience of Love
Jim Moore

The Porcelain Apes of Moses
Mendelssohn
Jean Nordhaus

Song of the World Becoming:
New and Collected
Poems 1981–2001
Pattiann Rogers

Atlas
Katrina Vandenberg

MILKWEED EDITIONS

Founded in 1979, Milkweed Editions is the largest independent, nonprofit literary publisher in the United States. Milkweed publishes with the intention of making a humane impact on society, in the belief that good writing can transform the human heart and spirit. Within this mission, Milkweed publishes in five areas: fiction, nonfiction, poetry, children's literature for middle-grade readers, and the World As Home—books about our relationship with the natural world.

JOIN US

Milkweed depends on the generosity of foundations and individuals like you, in addition to the sales of its books. In an increasingly consolidated and bottom-line-driven publishing world, your support allows us to select and publish books on the basis of their literary quality and the depth of their message. Please visit our Web site (www.milkweed.org) or contact us at (800) 520-6455 to learn more about our donor program.

INTERIOR DESIGN BY CHRISTIAN FÜNFHAUSEN.

TYPESET IN FILOSOFIA.

PRINTED ON ACID-FREE 50# FRASER TRADE BOOK PAPER

BY FRIESEN CORPORATION.